Doing
My Best
to Shine

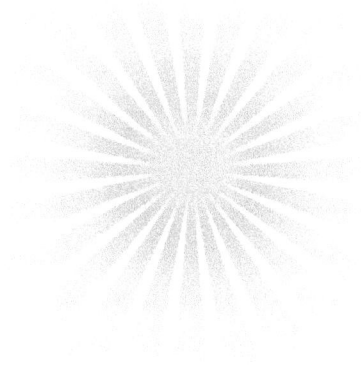

Doing My Best to Shine

poems by
David James

SHANTI ARTS PUBLISHING

BRUNSWICK, MAINE

Doing My Best to Shine

Published by Shanti Arts Publishing

Designed by Shanti Arts Designs

Cover image (front): Smileus / # 340231219/ stock.adobe.com

Shanti Arts LLC
193 Hillside Road
Brunswick, Maine 04011
shantiarts.com

Printed in the United States of America

ISBN: 978-1-962082-54-9 (softcover)

Library of Congress Control Number (LCCN): 2024948877

For all those whose light has shown me the way, I love you.

CONTENTS

That Stunned Look on My Face

ACKNOWLEDGMENTS

Bourgeon: "What We Learn of Faith"

Bryant Literary Review: "When Fall Arrives"

Cloudbank: "Perchakucha Divided by Four"

Colere: "Making a Case for Selling Your Soul"

Doubly Mad: "Bidding War"

Emergence Anthology: "Fourteen Pounds"

Escape into Life: "The Art of Subtraction" and "Even Miracles Begin with Desire"

Green Hills Literary Lantern: "All Things"

Illuminations: "Forget the Real One"

Last Stanza Poetry Journal: "Big Love"; "A Matter of Time"; "Not What I Planned"; "One Lovely Day at a Time"; "Q and A"; and "Research that Matters #19"

Michigan Roots (anthology): "A Day like This"

One Sentence Poems: "I Wouldn't Be Afraid"

Poetry East: "A Common Theology" and "Tasting God"

Qua: "A Novel View of the World"

Rabble Review: "No One Knew Who I Was"

Sheila-Na-Gig: "I Suppose the Cells are Splitting into Something We Cannot Know"

Spank the Carp: "I'm a God"

Sparks of Calliope: "Opening My Fist"

Talking River Review: "Final Exam"

Third Wednesday: "Somedays the Bear"

Train River Anthology: "Nothing to Laugh About"

Uppagus: "The Theology of Doubt"

Westminster Art Festival: "A Little Relief"

What Rough Beast: "On Certain Days"

When It Rains, It Pours (anthology): "Let it Rain"

A Common Theology

TASTING GOD ✦

It's so easy to believe
there's a God behind

and because and beyond
all this beauty.

You'd have to be blind
to ignore the sleeve

of blue sky,
the maple trees dancing in wind,

clouds swimming overhead.
The miracles of every morning

sit down and open
in plain view for any eye

to see. Some say it's nonsense to think
there's a God, a creation force, a power

beneath and behind the world,
but I'm on the side of belief.

When I stare outside, I can feel the rain showers
blowing in from the west. I lick my lips and prepare to drink.

ALL THINGS ✦

Since no one can
tell me
what happens after my heart bursts into flames,
my breath into sand,
my limbs into soggy bones,

I'll drink this tea,
slurp this cabbage soup, watch the leaves
turn red and gold as they fall
and become devotees
to all things unknown,

all things that move and weave
under stars,
all things that glow down here
and force me to believe
that I am not

alone.

ONE LOVELY DAY AT A TIME ✦

sitting in the back yard,
a cool breeze rustling the leaves,
the drone of an airplane above,
watching four cherry tomatoes slowly turn orange
on the plant

and I forget the ease
with which it could all vanish,
swept away or burned, everything going black
with a massive aneurysm,

like my uncle who sits at home
waiting for his to burst and bleed out.
in some ways, I hope he has a heart attack
in his sleep—a quiet, quick departure.

how do you greet the new morning
knowing it could be a matter of hours or days
before your world goes silent?

i guess you savor this piece of toast,
enjoy that glass of grapefruit juice,
smile when your grandson
brings in a crayon drawing
of a mighty dragon
with your name
on it.

FOURTEEN POUNDS ✦

for Debbie, Kevin, Peg, Colleen, Al, Molly, and Jon

my brother and I head out to the garage
to put your ashes in the urn.

besides the one large urn, we have four
small ornamental ones for your children, a token
to place on a shelf. we have so much to learn
as we march toward

the end. when we dump the bag of ashes,
your dust floats up and we breathe you
into our lungs. your eighty-two years on earth
has burned down to fourteen pounds. Kevin sprinkles a dash

of salt in each urn and places a single .22
bullet inside to signify your love of hunting and guns.
next week, we'll bury you in the veteran's cemetery
with a brief military service. we'll tell stories again,

laugh and cry, give big bear hugs to anyone
who comes. we'll do whatever's necessary
to honor your presence in our lives. you're here,
Dad, in our bones, our hearts, our words, our hairlines.

and some day when we least expect it,
your voice will rise up in us, so real and so clear.

A COMMON THEOLOGY ✦

my faith
is a clear blue sky with one hawk floating up there
so high
I have to squint
to see it.
it's my dream,
my voice, my pocket full of change,
my good cigar, my confidence
that the seeds
I planted yesterday
will rise
and grow.

my faith
is a fuchsia hanging under the robin's nest,
purple flowers reaching toward earth.
it's a glass
of Japanese tea,
a freshly cut lawn,
a midnight
thunderstorm,
that feeling inside when you know someone
loves you
for who you are
and not what you can be.

A HILL TO STAND ON (NOT) ✦

we all have to die, that's clear,
that's known,

but we don't have to invite the reaper
into our lungs by covering our ears
and ignoring science. if people want to fall
on that hill and claim they're not drones,
that's their right.

let them drink bleach and swallow horse pills.
let them fear vaccine infertility, believe 5G phone
towers spray invisible diseases all
over the land.

                       maybe in hindsight,
we should have
tried harder, argued more, reasoned with our neighbors
to follow some logic, to delight
in common sense rather than crawl
down another rabbit hole and get blown away like chaff
into empty fields.

we can choose life or choose the hospital ICU
and a thirty percent chance to live. we can laugh
and hug safely, or we can defend the choice to fall
                          and die alone.

OPENING MY FIST ✦

1

the life and death of me
sleeps upstairs

in his crib, a towel for a blanket.
Henry, my youngest grandchild,
dreams
about pieces of toast the size of cars
          swimming in a sea

of lemon rice soup.
my heart falls out
when he smiles at me

or says, "Wow, oh, wow."

we spent an hour this morning
climbing up the stairs,
climbing back down.

2

there are no words pure enough
for the love
of my three grandchildren.

they are my personal gold mines,
my new stars, oceans yet undiscovered,
glorious miracles.

3

I turn 60 next week
and already find myself calculating

how much time I have left
      to see them graduate, marry, have kids of their own,

struggle to lift the weight
of the future

off my tired back

4

which they will not be able to do,
of course.

5

life is an opening of your fist
and a letting go.

you give away pieces of yourself here,
lose small pieces there, and hope
someone sees them,

picks them up, maybe even keeps them,
tucked away
in a dresser, a glove compartment,

a hole in the back yard.

borges was right—a man dies for real
only
when the last person
in the world

who remembers him

dies.

6

I have seventeen years left,
if the lousy actuaries know what they're doing.

maybe I can prove them wrong.

7

maybe
not.

WHAT WE LEARN OF FAITH ✦

for Nick Bozanic

is to trust the heart.
It's like a trout in the river,
swimming with ease
and confidence, hunkering down
under a fallen tree
to rest.

Sometimes it breaks
the surface, leaping into sunlight,
splashing back
into the water,
gone, quiet, invisible,
but there. Always there.

REINCARNATION: A PLEA ✦

Listen: I want to come back
as a hawk, banking against a belly of clouds
the size of New Jersey.

I want another chance to grab
the day by the horns, crowd
out any hint of fear and plea
with God for forgiveness.

Mine was a life made out of mud—
no silver, no gold, no precious stones.

I opened my eyes each morning, guessed
at a direction and walked into the flood,
drowning with the least of them,
one wasted day after another.

Look out through my weeping eyes
and you'll see the world condemned,
left to rot and smother
in self-pity. I know now there's more.

Let me glide on shafts of sunlight,
turn and dive toward the earth with faith
that I'll kill, eat, rejoice, lift my wings and soar.

EVEN MIRACLES BEGIN WITH DESIRE ✦

for Keith Taylor

It's been weeks with no hummingbird.

The feeder's full, hanging near the hibiscus.
There's nothing to do but watch and wait,

hoping the tiny bird gets the word
that nectar's here and it's free.
It's like life: somewhere miracles did

and still do occur. Consider yourself blessed
when you find one or one finds you.
That's when the unexplained, what's hid-

den from view, what's lost, is seen.
As if by request
a hummingbird darts by the feeder,

hovers, drinks, and flies away.
The whole thing takes five seconds or less,

time enough to bow, bend a knee.

SOMETHING UP MY SLEEVE ✦

For my next trick,

I'll follow every living thing
that's ever graced the earth

into the ground.
I can see the end of the pier,

hear the click
of the coffin shut;

I can do the math
because it's all subtraction from this point on.

At my age, it's one take away
after another. The short end of the stick

is in my pocket and there's no way
to turn back the clocks.

This is where faith comes in—
I can face the end with dignity since I've built

a road to heaven in my heart, brick by golden brick.

A DAY LIKE THIS ✦

"Dust is king."
—George Hitchcock

On days like this,

I can deny anything. The maple leaves glow
in sunlight while a cool wind

moves the trees,
large branches dipping in a slow
dance for no one but me. By the skin

of my teeth, I'm lucky to have made it this far.
I have no real complaints, at least
none worth mentioning. Everyone has regrets,
disappointments, those moments when my beliefs were jarred

and the ugly beast
of doubt rose up to shake my world apart.
I learned to glue it back together somehow.
I learned to go on until a day like this

opens up around me and I start
to think I can live forever, that every tree bough
waves to me, that the sky's blue is mine

to keep. There are ripe tomatoes in the garden,
six peppers and a few cucumbers left. I'm going to ignore the dust

and do my best to shine.

A MATTER OF TIME ✦

"I was lugging my death from Kampala to Krakow."
—C. K. Williams, "The Coffin Store"

Every morning when I set my feet on the ground,
death wakes and climbs on my back.

I can't feel him or her, but the older I get
the more I know I'm lugging around

that final gasp, baked into my DNA.
On a park bench, in a cute, little vacation shack

on the big lake, in a hotel room along I-69,
my day will arrive.

I'll bargain and pray, hoping against hope for some slack
in the rules but fail. Like everyone.

So savor the tortellini and the smell of the rind
as you peel a sweet mandarin. Revel in your son's laugh,

the new mums on the porch, two jays fighting at the bird feeder.
When the first leaves turn red, I don't think of it as a dire sign.

I smile like a baby and look everywhere with my eyes of clay.

THE ART OF SUBTRACTION ✦

Over a matter of years and deliberate stupidity,

I've learned to live with my mistakes,
even relish in them.
The end doesn't care about my stock or pedigree:
that final moment is the same for everyone.

Over the course of a life and sporadic heartbreaks,
I've developed my own brand of vision:
I see what I want and ignore the rest.
It's probably the best way to shake

the blues and bask in some kind of glory.
With so little time down here and none
of the answers, I've decided to dance and sing,

wrestle and eat, toast the hours left and right
and care less about a reason.

The sun rises and falls. I can take a hint.

MAKING A CASE FOR SELLING YOUR SOUL ✦

I'll make the deal, sign on the dotted line
if it'll buy me a few more years of breathing.

Just name the down payment, I'll pay it.
When you get to my age, you see how the sunlight shines

through the trees and leaves, on the water, through the eyes
of your grandchildren and your heart starts pleading

for more time. I see a far more beautiful world beneath
the one I'm walking in. Every bird sings to me,

every peony glows, every sunset, bleeding
across the horizon, uses its color to pry

open my skull, shake my brain free of deceit
or pride. Now that I understand what matters,

I'm not afraid to live. Give me each new day like a baby bird
in my hands. I'll keep her warm, protect her, feed her, teach

her everything I know until she rises up on her own
                    and flies.

ONE WEEKEND IN DECEMBER ✦

My five year-old grandson Elliot
makes a flame-thrower out of Tinker Toys
and lights me up.
"You're dead, Papa," he says
with a smile.

Annie, three, holds a laser
that pierces any force-field
or shield. I slump over in my chair,
dead again.

The metaphor does not
escape me. As my grandkids grow,
I walk closer to the edge.
It's not that they're here
to kill me (though they all do
with their homemade guns),
it's just a natural fact.

Of my six grandchildren,
I'll be lucky to attend two or three
of their weddings
before the lights go out.

Elliot locks me in jail,
handcuffed with several beaded
Mardi Gras necklaces
before setting me on fire.

Annie has re-worked her laser
  into a long knife. She pushes it into my chest.
"I'm stabbing you in the heart, Papa.
  I'm stabbing you." I make a pained grunt,
  drop my head to one side while she giggles.

And yes, I feel the cut,
  my heart bleeding for more time,
  my arms reaching to hug her close
  until she cries out
  and I let go. She stabs me again
  for good measure
  and then runs into the kitchen
  to kill her grandma.

You Can't Help but Wonder

I SUPPOSE THE CELLS ARE SPLITTING
INTO SOMETHING WE CANNOT KNOW ✦

after the last line of a poem by Jack Ridl

Everything breaks

                    into something else, which breaks again—
                        a wristwatch into a messy divorce;
                a phone call into a drunken binge, twenty stitches,
                        and a lost wallet; a smile into a yes;
        some old incense into a baby girl, born prematurely, five pounds,

too small to take home yet.
Every cell down here melts and decays and grows
into that cardinal, that flag, that broken tree limb, this snow
        piled up
above the mailbox, that lovely inch of skin on the woman's back
that no one has ever kissed,

                                    or touched.

BIDDING WAR ✦

after James Tate

"I saved a baby wren today," I tell Roger, though he didn't ask
and I know he hates birds. "I saved a koala bear stuck on my
roof," he says. "After the wren rescue," I say, "I saved a sperm
whale, gave it mouth-to-mouth, then pushed it back into the
ocean." I couldn't let him out-save me. "Well," says Roger,
"once the koala was safe, I pulled a rhino out of Keller's well,
reattached his horn using Gorilla Glue and rode him back
to Africa. To the motherland." "Now that's bullshit," I say.
"You can't ride a rhino across the Atlantic." "You can't push a
whale into the ocean from Fenton, Michigan, either," Roger
replies. "Have you ever heard of Meister Eckhart?" I ask.
"No," he says. "He's a monk from the 1300s. He said if you can
imagine doing it, then you have done it in the eyes of God."
Roger smiles. "Then I rode a rhino across the Atlantic."

That's when I picture drowning Roger in his pool, and I know
I've won.

MY SLAM POEM ✦

If I was a slam poet,
you wouldn't be reading this.
I'd be up on a stage
performing my work,
allowing my words to act out
and turn my mouth into a fist,
my voice into a play.

And when I was finished,
I'd close the page in my memory
and throw the poem to the floor.
There's no container big enough,
no cage strong enough to hold it for a day
or even an hour.

My poem would run along the shore,
splashing and laughing, wind blowing
its long hair back.
My slam poem would dissolve into the waves
and return as an eagle
ready to rise and soar
until I perform again,
and you become
its delicious prey.

NO RHYME AND NO REASON ✦

Not a cloud in the sky,

shades of blue up there as far as I can see,
and I'm sitting on the porch,
six flower pots blooming around me,
smoking a cigar, drinking iced tea, writing a poem

      while people in Ukraine struggle for freedom and die,
      Sudan implodes into the newest international crisis,
      millions live through drought
      or the lack of clean water,

      while one dictator after another
      grabs power and crucifies
      their opponents.
      Something's wrong with this picture.

There are men, women and children
starving, getting massacred, running for their lives,
and I'm lounging in the sun in front of my house,
wondering what kind of fish for dinner

to fry.

Q AND A ✦

"Hedge wizards and makers of almanacs, UFO abductees and 5G truthers, all hold out the same promise—that one universal hidden truth shall be revealed, and the horror of not knowing will come to an end."
—Hari Kunzru, "Complexity," *Harper's Magazine*, January 2021

It's raining on December 21 and I don't know why.
Jupiter and Saturn align tonight
into what might have been the star
of Bethlehem, and maybe it was, but we'll never know.

Most days, I shake my head and sigh,
not sure what to do or what to believe.
The truth is a moving target, one moment in Qatar,
the next week in Detroit. Tomorrow, it's flying low
over Lake Huron before landing on the Isle of Wight.

Maybe there is no hidden truth and we've been deceived
by our own simplistic thinking. Maybe we
should consider the concept of truth like snow—
each flake unique and beautiful, each truth a sight
for sore eyes: the truth of fire and a Cuban cigar,
the truth of pumpkin pie, the truth of the acorn or flea
or red cardinal on the fence post on a snowy day.

Maybe truth is everywhere and nowhere. The light
shines down from the planets whether we're standing in the yard
or asleep in bed. The world performs and we're in the show
for such a short time: be happy to grab any old truth and stay.

A NOVEL VIEW OF THE WORLD ✦

"24. There is no clean narrative line."
—Dennis Hinrichsen, "[Fission]"

Don't we all want to make sense of this
    day/life/death/universe?
    We want to travel from point A to point B
    to get to point C for lunch. We want the hero
    (i.e., us) to encounter conflict and obstacles/
    to put up a fight until/the twist
    at the end/we come to the final battle/decision/action
to reach the holy grail/all under 120 minutes.

If only our lives were movies or plays
    or three-day bluegrass festivals. If we could accept this job/
    marry him or her/buy that house/raise these children/all
        sans risk/
    we'd die of boredom. We'd die with our soft hands
    and weak hearts/our dreams crumbling like feta/
    our short little lives/plotless/pointless/
    a drop in the river of a narration so bizarre/so complex/
all the years we've lived would add up to one sloppy kiss.

WHATEVER ✦

*"Thirty headless goats were found floating
in the Chattahoochee River."*
—Rafil Kroll-Zaidi, "Findings,"
Harper's Magazine, January 2022

Maybe it's just a coincidence, something chalked up
to chance, one of those strange anomalies

that occurs
every five-hundred years. In 2522, maybe they'll find
thirty human livers washed ashore in the Dead Sea.

Some suggest a satanic ritual, a bloody way to transfer
animal instinct into people by eating the brains

of a goat.
Maybe it's a sign of the apocalypse, the initial sacrifice
preceding God's judgment and slaughter of the profane.

Whatever it is, it's sick. I read this as a footnote
in a popular magazine, but it's one of millions

of facts
that makes me wonder why and how this world stays afloat.
Who decides, one day, that we're done?

THE SCIENCE OF POETRY ✦

"A good chemist is twenty times as useful as any poet."
—Ivan Turgenev, *Fathers and Sons*

My parents always said,
"Why don't you become an accountant
or engineer, or better yet, a chemist?"

I could be creating a cure for balding,
a drug to eliminate hangovers,
some potion to help me remember names.
I could be experimenting with new toxins
for household cleaners,
conjuring up a medicine to extend
the lives of comatose patients.

Where did I go wrong?

Look at my hands: they're too clumsy
for test tubes and microscopes.
They're useless when it comes
to Bunsen burners.

My parents have forgiven me
or, at least, learned to live without a chemist
in the family.
But I try in my own way
to make up for it, mixing letters into words,
dreaming of an elementary reaction
to get inside you,

to chart a path
toward that invisible chemical heart.

MERCY ✦

for Barbara

We're watching my mother-in-law
die. She doesn't know she's dying

because she has dementia, and my father-in-law
refuses to let anyone remind her

by saying the "c" word, cancer.

Some disagree with him but others applaud
the decision as touching and tender.

Just let her think she's losing weight,
that the pain in her shoulder is arthritis,

her lack of appetite due to inactivity.

What some see as a flaw,
others describe as loving compassion—

let her come to the end with blind ignorance

instead of repeating she has cancer
ten or twelve times a day, and each time,

watching her face contort, her jaw
drop. It seems kinder, gentler, to commit a little fraud

and let a white lie live
outside the few brain cells
she can still call her own.

A RIPE OLD AGE ✦

When you get this far by luck or accident, it's like being at the end
of a huge pier

and you find yourself looking down, seeing movies of your
        life under
the clear water—there's you with two grandsons on a train;
there's your wedding day; a surgery; your first house; over here

you're at a bluegrass music festival. You're in a garden, picking
        cucumbers
and tomatoes; walking through a rain forest; toasting in Ireland

with a couple you love; climbing over a stone wall
into a park. There's your son's birth, your daughter's, your son's;
here you are at work; there with your granddaughter

on a merry-go-round. In broken vignettes, the years sprawl
and swirl in front of you, motion pictures, still photographs,

some with sound, some with action. Before too long, you'll be
wondering how it all happened, where it went, and why are you
drifting in the open sea on some puny wooden raft?

ASK AND YOU SHALL RECEIVE ✦

"Whatever you ask in my name, this I will do."
—John 14:13 (ESV)

Jesus, can you give back the lives of the eight
people killed at the Allen Mall in Texas?
How about the six murdered in Ocean Springs?
Or the four massacred in Vicksburg, the four in Chicago,
the four in Atlanta, all in one week?

Will you lift the sorrow, Jesus, erase the great
pain from the hearts of mothers and fathers,
wives and husbands, lovers, sisters and brothers?

Can you please perform background checks, deny
the purchase of AR-15's, build reliable mental hospitals,
shield all children and clean the broken slate
in their minds, blessing them with innocence
by the mere wave
of your divine hand?

Our prayers don't seem to work, Lord.
Whatever you had planned for us is too late.

NOTHING TO LAUGH ABOUT ✦

It's broad daylight when a priest, a rabbi and a virus walk into a bar. The priest orders merlot, the rabbi, a martini, dry, and the virus, a Corona, nineteen of them. They all laugh at the obvious, how blatant the virus is to get shit-faced drunk. Though it's a non-smoking establishment, virus fires up a cigar. Who's going to kick him out? Who's going to tell him to stop the mayhem?

The priest and rabbi start arguing about the afterlife— the quality of conveniences and luxuries in their separate views of heaven after dying. The priest is certain there will be unlimited ice cream; the rabbi confirms a 24-hour deli with free fountain drinks. The virus, on his tenth beer already, knows they're both wrong but doesn't want to condemn. They'll find out the truth soon enough, he thinks.

"So, Viro," says the rabbi, "tell us what your heaven looks like—lots of hand-wringing and sighing?"

The priest raises his glass and says, "Or do you just keep passing it back and forth to each other?" The two men laugh, finish their drinks, order a second.

Now on his fifteenth beer, virus belches and replies, "Here's what I know about dying." He kisses them both on the mouth, downs four more beers and staggers out onto the sidewalk, squinting in the light, not feeling a damn thing.

RESEARCH THAT MATTERS #19 ✦

"Frequent travel makes people happier by 7 percent."
—Rafil Kroll-Zaidi, "Findings,"
Harper's Magazine, January 2022

If you trim your toenails
once a month,
you will live, on average, 1.2 years longer
than those who trim toenails every six months.

Eating breakfast in bed,
even sporadically, makes a couple
feel eleven percent closer.

Having your own vegetable garden,
regardless of the type of vegetables planted,
will cause your hair to turn gray
at a slower pace than normal.

Being kissed at least three times daily
allows you to remember your good dreams at night
at a rate 6.7 percent greater than
those left unkissed.

And for some unknown reason,
people who remember their good dreams
are better drivers, smile more often,
leave larger tips, and touch the faces
of their loved ones whenever they can
or whenever it's appropriate.

AFTER FORTY-FIVE YEARS OF MARRIAGE ✦

Me: Do you want me to read you a love poem?
My wife: No, just go to Kroger's.

Sometimes food is the salve, the medicine
for sadness and grief. Not a hug or kiss,
not a promise or words of love,
but the essentials—milk, tea, bread and eggs,
yogurt, Brussel sprouts, bananas.

　　Let the musicians, guitars in
hand, create their songs and lyrics
to move our hearts.

　　Let the painters set up their easels
and capture life in full bloom
so we can imagine where joy begins.

　　And let the poets write sonnets
and epics to say what
cannot be said with a human voice.

Sometimes nothing helps more than a BLT
on toasted wheat bread, the mayonnaise spread sure and thin.

RECIPE FOR HATE ✦

Gather up ten thumb tacks,
a dozen nails, one dull razor blade,
some dog shit, a small screwdriver
and swallow them all.

In a clear glass, mix together a shot of kerosene,
quarter cup of rye Sazerac,
seven drops of tractor oil and a tablespoon
of arsenic. Drink it down in one gulp.

Wait for three days without leaving your house
or apartment. Then take a knife
and carve a slice down the back
of your left arm:

if no blood appears,
you're ready. Now you can hate
anything or anyone for any reason.
Or no reason. Your heart's dying
to attack.

NO ONE KNEW WHO I WAS ✦

after a first line by James Tate

not even me. I was a clear
slate, an empty shoebox, a tricycle
with no wheels, a tree
with roots made entirely
of cheap blue yarn. And I didn't even
own a pair of knitting needles.
       Every morning I woke up
to a slap in the face;
every night I fell asleep
with a handful of rocks
under my pillow. I'd wave
to people walking past my house
but no one waved back,
no one glanced in my direction.
       Maybe I was dead, or a ghost,
or maybe I came from
another dimension that gave me
the power of invisibility, the gift
of the anonymous millionaire donor
who is able to secretly help people
get through their darkest moments,
able to watch what happens
yet not be bothered by all
the groveling thanks and sincere
gratitude and hero worship.
       Talk about freedom. I can
walk into any coffee shop or bar
or drugstore and no one looks up,
no one remembers,
no one ever says,
"Hey, don't I know you?"

THE THEOLOGY OF DOUBT ✦

"The blessings of doubt have not excused us from the burdens of faith."
—Joshua Ferris, *To Rise Again at a Decent Hour*

There's doubt under my fingernails.

Each morning, I swallow two pills
of white doubt to make it
through another day.
It takes more than willpower
to stay alive. Most people fake it,
pretending to hold their beliefs
high above the actual truth. Not me.
I breathe in my doubt
and accept the worry and grief
as necessary evils, as something I need
in order to be human.

Look, if I was blind
and faith opened my eyes to perfect sight,
I'd fall to my knees, born again.
But doubt would slide in behind
my prayers, seep into one brain cell,
then another. Then fourteen.

You'd be able to see doubt creeping into my face,
filling me with just a little bit of hell.

That Stunned Look on My Face

LET IT RAIN ✦

I love that rain, that easy rain

when the bees are still out,
hovering from flower to flower,
some of the pollen
falling to the ground. I have no doubt
bees feel a certain pleasure,
a rain drop here, their feet wet,
  a bee shower
as they climb on each stamen.
I imagine the bees smile a bit
as they hover in the drizzle,
pulled from one flower to another,
forgetting why they exist, but doing their job
because it's what bees do.

If I listen closely, it's their singing I hear.

ON CERTAIN DAYS ✦

for Marc Sheehan

"Brothers and sisters, never tire of doing what is good."
— 2 Thessalonians 3:13

the world crashes
& burns
& you burn with it.
everything you've done ends in a pile of ashes
& the wind
scatters you home. this is how you learn
to take nothing for granted.

some days the world slaps you
in the face and has no concern
for who you are or who you know.
you stand there & take it, no shred
of honor, no handful of hope.

there are even days when the world
wants nothing more than your head
on a platter, your body skinned
& quartered, hung from rope
tied to any bare tree.

so much is out of your control,
beyond the scope
of your sorrow.
some days, your dignity
lies in a warm bucket of shit.
but then, every once in a while,

the world stops, falls to its knees
& lets you win:
every pitch thrown, you hit
out of the park;
every bird sings your name;
every star in the dark sky, lit
& shining, smiles down on you

                       until your heart glows.

BIG LOVE ✦

I ended up dissecting love again
after living 43 years married to the same woman.

On a table wiped clean with alcohol,
I cut our love open down the middle,
spread it apart, to find this:

> a thimbleful of red tears
> a whoopee cushion
> two four-leaf clovers
> a palmful of forgiveness that looked like granola
> several Ahmad tea bags
> recipes for biscotti and cracker-toffee
> dozens of unused theatre tickets
> a blow-up water lounge
> two golf balls

It smelled like patience,
like understanding,
and after I sewed it shut,
the stitches dissolved completely
as it healed itself.

Every year, I dissect love
trying to determine
how it works, how it stays and grows,
and each year
my list is different.

Last year, I found yarn,
notebooks, eggnog, a bear hug, a kilt,
mango hard cider, darts, corned beef and cabbage.

The year before there were Christmas ornaments,
fuchsia petals, several fat quarters, a book of poems,
baby clothes, a half-cup of marvel
with some wonder sprinkled on top.

Each dissection
is unpredictable, and each one surprises me,
but I've decided to stop.
I haven't figured out
a damn thing about love,
other than
there's no map or secret to it,
no magic trick or potion.

            It's snow falling, a bluebird in the maple,
        the perfect gin and tonic, the smell of your hair,
          an almost full moon in the cloudless sky,
             a dog barking across the golf course,
              the chimes ringing at the bottom
                 of the stairs as I wake up
                    to find you
                      lying
                      beside
                       me.

NOT WHAT I PLANNED ✦

First of October and the leaves flame up red
on the big maple out back,

unlike in California where the flames are real,
houses and wineries burning to dust, the dead

count rising daily. No, this flame
is metaphorical and unfortunate when you stack

it up against the reality of climate change.
Doesn't it feel like the world is spinning

out of control? Like God is smoking crack
in some basement, unable to claim

his kingdom or answer our prayers or even arrange
to have the fires put out. Toss in a cup of economic despair,

a handful of racial division, and two buckets of COVID,
and you can't help but feel deranged.

This was going to be an autumn poem where I proclaimed
the beauty of dying leaves as they glow in the crisp air,

but it's turned dark; it's turned real.
Look, this world has been falling apart since the beginning,

but we've learned how to ignore the signs and stare
at the glorious sunset. It may be the only way to stay sane.

FINAL EXAM ✦

after Toi Derricotte

You're standing closer
to the edge
every year. Every day, really.

You know where this will end
and you have no say
in the matter.

It could be next Tuesday
or seven years from tomorrow.
It could be decades

but you *will* fall.
What should you do
when you're near the cliff's edge,

and there's nowhere to go but down?
A.   Ignore the facts and pretend there's no cliff.
B.   Take a big running jump.

C.   Enjoy the day, love those around you
      and piss in the eye of fate.
D.   None of the above.

LIKE IN REAL LIFE ✦

Because the sky was a beautiful blue,
I knew
the next day would never arrive.

God glanced down and said,
"The dead will melt away. My right arm of chance
will lift you
out of the muck you have created."

I closed my eyes
so my heart would open.

With a running start,
I leaped into the wind and floated away.
No one would miss me, much.

Like in real life, I tumbled and turned,
drifted and fell, never knowing where I was going to land.

It's all a big game
except we use stones, bottle caps and leaves
instead of knights, queens and kings,

and we use hope and dreams instead
of strategy and time.

If I knew what happened to the winners
once they're buried,

I might be able to change the stunned look on my face.

FORGET THE REAL ONE ✦

Now that our children have married, moved away,
are creating lives without us, or at least,
with no need for us, what's left?

The house shrinks into a few rooms, but we won't betray
the past by throwing out old trophies and dolls,
clothes, that oboe and cornet. These might be

used by the grandkids someday. We eat out
more than we ever did. It's something to do.
Three weekends in a row, we've gone to see

plays, caught up in someone's pretend life and forget
the real one for a few sweet hours. We could shout
obscenities toward God; we could lie

to ourselves; we could imagine
the world crumbling forward without
us, which it will. But what's true

and what's desire is hard to accept, harder to deny.
No one has any power over the end.
It'll come whenever it damn well pleases.

Stars fall from the sky.
Hearts break and blow away in the wind.

SOMEDAYS THE BEAR ✦

for Preacher Roe

Sometimes you eat the bear and sometimes
the bear eats you. Either way, it's a bloody mess.

The snow's falling—four inches or more—
and there you are, skinning a bear like a crime
scene, hacking away
at the fur, slicing the carcass,
searching for bear sirloin and ribs. Next week,

it could be you sprawled on the ground,
torn apart, chewed, digested.

If only you knew when it was going to be your day.

You could wake up and head out like a Greek
god, fearless and beautiful. You could grab the sun,
throw a dozen stars in your mouth,
climb to the peak
of any mountain. There will be bear fillets

on the grill tonight. Tomorrow, no one
knows. And that's the point: you win some,
lose some, tie some. Then you order dim sum
and enjoy the hot mustard and plum
sauce, savor the tea, before it all goes away.

I WOULDN'T BE AFRAID ✦

if you
told me
death
would be
this simple,
that the end
would ease
me into
the afterlife
like a clock
winding down
quietly,
gently,
if you could
guarantee me
a sweet kiss
in that final
second before
my last
breath,
if I knew
you would
go on
and enjoy
your days
and memories,
revel in
the morning sun
with your cup
of Ahmad tea
and knitting,
our grandchildren

coming over
to visit
and swim,
their smiles
planted on
your full heart,
I'd close
my eyes
and let
my soul
go, let it
swirl
around you
and touch
your face
one more
time
before
climbing
the golden
stairs to
heaven where
I'd save a
cloud for you
and a perfect
set of wings,
waiting there
at the pearly gates
with hand-picked
flowers and a
glorious
smile.

WHEN FALL ARRIVES ✦

Fall in four days and another year
winds down to a grinding stop.
The apples ripen in the sun
while the Serrano peppers implode.
The fuchsia sends out its last blooms
for the frantic bees.
One blink and the trees will be on fire,
blowing apart like IED's,
cutting the truth across our hearts.
Another blink and the world will be buried
in white, frozen and invisible for months.

✦ ✦ ✦

The glory days come and go like memories,
lost at the end of my fingertips.
I reach out and grab air.
Last night, I misplaced the harvest moon
in a clear sky of stars.
It was there, I swear to you,
and when I went to show my wife,
it was gone.

✦ ✦ ✦

I take nothing for granted anymore:
waking up, drinking sake, staring into the sweet face
of my first grandchild, one week old.
As he sleeps in my arms,
he smiles, or at least it looks like that.

I remember my Uncle Darrel's words
from another life: "Look, he's talking to the angels."

✦ ✦ ✦

Four days when fall arrives,
there will be no way to keep it here.
I find myself talking to the angels:
be with my family, watch over us,
keep this baby safe and strong and healthy,
give us this day
                  what we don't deserve.

YES, ANOTHER AUTUMN POEM ✦

Let's get this out of my system—the autumn poem

that arrives every October, on schedule, as leaves
turn in a color bucket, blaze out orange and red before falling
and blowing across lawns and parking lots, finding homes
in every nook and cranny. Such an old metaphor,
it still works and seems reasonable. Though it's naïve
to compare human life to trees shedding, standing bare
against the elements, it's an apt image for a man
who sees his days numbered and memory slipping, who grieves
how little time he spends with the grandkids he adores.
If I had my way, I'd hug and kiss them daily; I'd be there
at band concerts and soccer games and dance recitals,
cheering them on.

But life doesn't always work out the way I want.

Leaves fall, rain crashes down, and my prayers
rise up in the cold wind, scattering like spores
across the heavens. It took sixty years to realize I'm a pawn
in a chess game that never ends. The trees strip down
and shake their anorexic arms at the stars. I feel parts of me
coming loose, crumbling away. It won't be long

before the cold winds blow and we wash up on some distant shore.

A MINOR MIRACLE ✦

This is one of those windy days,

big clouds in a blue sky,
that can convince you you'll live forever,
never aging, never losing your hair,
not an ache to be found on your body.

Usually, you're stumbling your way through a maze
of deadlines and disappointments, zoom calls
and emails, wondering how the hell
you'll ever get the lawn cut or laundry done.

Not today. Today you're a minor deity
under the radar of all the big guns, amazed
at how close the birds come to you sitting
on the front porch, your garden blooming with radishes
and acorn squash, sunflower and corn. When you glance up
to the heavens, you swear you can see a face

so you bow your head and give praise.

A LITTLE RELIEF ✦

The sky this morning
won't give up
its rain.
The trees stand perfectly still,
leaves pointing to the dark clouds,
praying for it. The flowers
bow down in the grayness
while birds
do what birds always do.

The air feels wet
as if the molecules could
spontaneously burst into droplets.

We've let the asparagus
grow wild, a good two feet
over the fence now.
My tomato plants have wilted,
    despite my steady watering.
Only the fuchsia, secure
in the shade, continues to bloom,
its red cherry flowers popping
like parachutes.

In a few weeks, God willing,
I'll celebrate my first full year
into the second half of a century
on this burning planet.

I'm trying to do my part, sitting
under the tree, apples dropping around me,
praying, like the rest of the world,
for some rain, a breeze, a sweet kiss on my neck,

some light to lead us
toward another chance.

I'M A GOD ✦

for Cloud, Chloe, Henry, Simon, Elliot, and Annie

I'm a god who rises
above the ground,
walks on water and trees,
grabs ears and finds prizes
of gum, mints, coins.

When I enter a room, the invisible crown
on my head glows.
"Papa!" they shout. *"Ji-chan!"*
and then the sound
of their feet running toward me.

Of course, I know
it won't last—time will draw
them to sports and friends, to books
and music, finally, into the throes
of lust and love, grinding into the messy real world.

But for now, I'll be a god and lift them in my grandpa
arms, rub their palms on my whiskers
until they squirm and laugh.
As long as they'll let me, I'll ignore my common flaws
and carry the universe on my shoulders.

ASSUMING GOD IS THERE ✦

let's assume God is up there crying tears
bigger than Lake Michigan
with every gunshot and explosion,
       with every
family forced to live on the streets, every person
walking in a dark place who hurts and hears
       that voice
inside telling them there's no reason to live anymore.

let's assume God sees the pain and suffering but is
       helpless,
depressed and angry. whether we like it or not, it appears
we're on our own, you know, free will and the
       power
to make or break what's left of these mistakes. let's assume
there's time to save ourselves, that God is praying
we grab the helm of this big old sinking ship
       and steer.

YEAH, AT THAT AGE ✦

i'm at that age where my friends
are retiring, where questions about health care
and whether we'll be able to afford it
in the future worry me.

have i saved enough money or will i be forced to wear
the Walmart greeter's jacket
and pretend i'm happy you've come to our store?
i'm at that age where my friends

are wintering in florida, where each day
feels like i'm drifting along in a boat without oars
as another storm slams the coast, the wind
picking up across the great sea.

the clocks shrink; each hour
loses a few seconds every week.
there's a certain urgency
in the morning as the new light devours

the day faster than i can
live it. i'm at that age where a darkness
stands in the shadows, at the far edge of the woods,
staring at me, rubbing its ancient hands.

PERCHAKUCHA DIVIDED BY FOUR ✦

Perchakucha is a Japanese presentation form which allows for twenty slides and twenty seconds per slide.

1

This day is made from hope, light, wind and a blue sky swirling around a few clouds traveling east. The cedars shake up and down, waving to me, so I wave back. I blow a kiss in their direction and they blush, not pink, but a lighter green. I love their smiles.

2

My four-year old grandson, Henry, is having a meltdown because he doesn't want to go home for dinner. His mother says, "Watch your attitude." His younger brother, Simon, announces, "I'm watching my attitude."
Then this sweet boy looks up to me, straight-faced, and asks, "What's an attitude?"

3

It's hard to believe it was 65 degrees today, March 27. T-shirt weather for Michiganders. But snow is predicted for the weekend, shocking the hell out of the robins.
I opened the windows to let spring in. We had some tea and biscuits and then she begged off, you know, buds to create, flowers to make.

4

Smoked two cigars today as I cut wood for shelves in the
basement, stained the mailbox for the first time in twenty
years. Finished a poem, revised another. Mahi-mahi for
dinner with a baked potato.
Sometimes I forget where I live and how blessed I am.

5

Half-moon up there, peeking behind wisps of clouds. A train
barrels through town, on schedule, its horn echoing off stars.
It's good to be in love after forty years, three kids, six grands,
and three parents still walking the earth. This day goes down
and, with luck, another's born into our open arms.

ABOUT THE AUTHOR

Born and raised on the third coast, Michigan, David James has published eight books and has had more than thirty of his one-act plays produced in the United States, Ireland, and England. After working for forty-five years in higher education, he retired in 2022.

www.ingramcontent.com/pod-product-compliance
Lightning Source LLC
Chambersburg PA
CBHW022039090426
42741CB00007B/1123